MW00585705

Dear Brothers

Dear Brothers

Letters Facing Death

RICHARD L. MORGAN,
HOWARD C. MORGAN,
AND JOHN C. MORGAN

RESOURCE *Publications* · Eugene, Oregon

DEAR BROTHERS
Letters Facing Death

Resource Publications
An Imprint of Wipf and Stock Publishers
199 W. 8th Ave., Suite 3
Eugene, OR 97401

www.wipfandstock.com

ISBN: 978-1-60899-275-1

Manufactured in the U.S.A.

Contents

Preface

It is not often that three brothers share their most personal stories about life and death with others. These letters were written over a year when each of us realized that the time ahead of us was limited. Rather than waiting until one of us passed from this earth, it would be wiser to share our insights sooner than later, a preparation for our own departures from this world if you will and a testimony for those we love who are left behind. And so began an exchange of letters that has dealt primarily with our hard won understandings of the meaning of death, which is to say really what living has meant to each of us.

While we share a rich Christian tradition, the grandsons of one famous preacher, G. Campbell Morgan, and one evangelist, Milford Hall Lyon, we've taken different paths.

Howard, a banker, facing the untimely losses of two wives and a daughter, has been a seminary board chair and now chair of the Interfaith Youth Corps. Richard, a Presbyterian minister and college teacher, is a writer often dealing with the spiritual issues of growing old. John, once a Unitarian Universalist minister, now teaches philosophy and ethics at an inner city community college.

Each of us shares a family tradition, but also different perspectives on the meaning of faith, especially when facing death. Richard and Howard tend to adopt a more Christian view, while John, a more skeptical one. Yet each of us accepts the other's point of view while at the same time being truthful of our own. We believe this offers a good model for a world often torn apart over religious issues. We seek common ground even while acknowledging differences.

Our initial intent in putting these letters together was to leave something behind for our family and friends. But as the letters seemed to point to a natural conclusion—each of our preferences for our own memorial services—we began to see that the informal, honest exchanges between us might be of use to others who struggle with some of the same questions we have brought to light. That is our simple hope and prayer.

Richard L. Morgan, Pittsburgh, Pennsylvania
Howard C. Morgan, Chicago, Illinois
John C. Morgan, Reading, Pennsylvania

Letters

August 19, 2008

Dear Brothers,

I sit here pondering the upcoming year and wondering what it will hold. I think as I near the three score years and ten mark, I am beginning to reflect more on the time remaining, wanting to make it meaningful.

I know my attitudes about life and death have changed a great deal ever since I almost died after surgery not long ago. One can reflect about the deaths of others and even one's own, but when death comes near you, everything takes on a deeper meaning. I know now that life is tenuous and death certain, so I need to make the most of the time I have left in a quiet preparation. One conclusion I have reached is that the best way to deal with death is to live well as long as it is physically possible.

I am both scared and curious about what—if anything—will happen after I die. Like most people, I don't want to endure a painful death. But as to what happens after I die, I have only hints. I know some people are certain they will live forever; I am not sure any longer I want eternity. Somehow knowing there is an end makes the journey from birth more, not less, important, for it is all we have.

One approach to facing death follows what Socrates the philosopher said as he neared his. If there is nothing beyond death, then, he said, he wouldn't know; and if there is something, he would not be afraid. This seems a reasonable attitude, although quite

3

honestly, when it comes to dying, I don't think reason rules: emotion does.

Plato, Socrates' pupil, was once asked to summarize his philosophy of life and he reportedly said: "practice dying." That summary seems strange at first, until one realizes that life and death are part of a process, that one makes the other meaningful and vice versa. It's like the yin and yang of Taoism—opposites sometimes are complementary.

Ah well, back to the reality of today, which is all I really have. I plan to get ready to teach, play my guitar, read a wonderful new book of short stories by a young American writer, go to the store, take a nap, and watch a baseball game tonight. Isn't ordinary life most important in the long run? As long as one's mind stays alert, learning to make each day count is the best lesson I learned from my encounter with death.

Shalom,

John

August 24, 2008

Dear Brothers,

Most people choose to fill their traveling years with conversation about the scenery, rather than the final destination. They either deny death or shove it under the table. Unfortunately it is disease, tragedy, or age that are the triggers that cause us to think about death. Since 1992, when I had a death skirmish following complications after surgery, death is very much on my mind. I became painfully aware that my life is short after I clicked on a website to see how many years I had left. The result was, "Sorry, your life has expired. Have a good day." Yeah, right.

I live in a retirement community of old people where the angel of death visits almost every month. I know that I feel the death of every person here, so my life is diminished every time a person's name appears on our memorial board.

Sure, I want to live more years, see my grandchildren graduate from college, attend their weddings (probably in a wheelchair), and hold my first great-great grandchild. I believe that there is still some work I can do before the end comes. But that may not be as I live in my eightieth year and know the sands of the hourglass are running out.

Like John, I am vitally concerned as to what happens when I die. Books about death and the life beyond are among the few left on my shelves. But all is speculation. The gates of heaven guard their secrets well, and few stray beams of light escape through the crevices, except . . . (more about that later).

Of the three of us, Howard, you have stared at death more in the loss of loved ones. You have been there for those "whom you have loved long since and lost awhile." I believe you can share a lot about this mystery we call death.

I love the Japanese saying, "The sunsets of life are just as beautiful as the sunrises." I have found this to be true in my later years. I hope that will be even truer when, "sunset and evening star" becomes my final song.[1]

Cheers,

Richard

1. Tennyson, "Crossing the Bar," line 1.

August 28, 2008

Dear Brothers,

It's not so difficult to reflect on death; but when it's *my* death, that's different! As you both know so well, I've seen more than my share of the deaths of loved ones who are our age—a sister, two wives, a daughter. It all seems unreal when I really focus on their disappearance. We expect to know death with older loved ones, family and friends, but to lose a contemporary, that's different.

In a real sense those traumatic deaths have helped me realize the reality of the end of life and "accept" the finality of its end on this earth as we know and love it. Often I wonder what the departed ones think about the moments of family life that we can't have them experience. I usually feel closeness at those times and a realization that they are seeing what is happening. We're just denied the capacity to see them.

Sometimes when I ponder these losses I wonder what on earth am I still doing here? It's an uncanny feeling that they remain connected to my persona—awareness that they are so close.

And so, do I look forward to my death? Uncertainty makes me unsure and I am driven by the joy of life and especially by my connection to those around me. If I could be certain of what happens after physical death—but, alas, that's no more possible than knowing the exact time of my death. Then I attach myself to faith and belief in the unknown, perhaps because of the beliefs of our parents. It's just hard for me to believe that an existence doesn't continue for those I love.

So, as life moves on beyond four score years and ten, these reflections become more of my psyche and my conscious thinking.

I still believe my favorite Woody Allen saying was that he didn't mind dying; he just didn't want to be there when it happened.

Be well,

Howard

August 30, 2008

Dear Brothers,

It's less than a month before the official start of autumn, a time of the year when change is in the air and when learning to deal with transitions is the name of the game. We took Jonathan off to college a week ago and left him. After being with us for eighteen years, I should have been prepared for how I felt—sad—but I wasn't. Cynthia had prepared for his leaving for months; I had not, so the loss was like a sudden death. He was here one day and gone the next, and his empty room left me grieving. I knew intellectually what was going on, but emotionally I was going through all the stages of loss.

A week later the grieving is still here but less intense. The grief comes and goes like I have always described to those mourning—in waves that never leave but diminish in intensity over time. The empty pit in my stomach is not here any longer, just an awareness that some rite of passage has taken place. And it has, both for my son and me. His rite of passage is leaving home and beginning to shape his own life. My rite is that of passing from being a sixty-seven-year-old parent to that of entering a later stage of life.

Two realities struck home this week and have given me pause to reflect.

Most of us can't really think of our own deaths; it's too difficult to take seriously that one day, one will cease to be. But, it's also clear that all along our life

9

journeys there are times of having to let go, to experience what I call "small deaths," and how we deal or fail to deal with these are rehearsals for the final exit.

The second realization is that each one of us is hopelessly self-absorbed, that the reason we fear death is that we fear the pain of dying and the loss of ourselves. The ego rules, even when we think otherwise. A few days after my son left home, I realized my sadness was as much about me as him; I was thinking of my loss, not his new adventure.

We'll be going to see Jonathan tomorrow to take him a few things he forgot to pack. It will be good to see him, but I also am aware that even after a week things will have changed. He's in a different place and on a new journey. Maybe if I think of death that way, it will be less threatening.

Cheers,

John

September 19, 2008

Dear Brothers,

Your letters have been meaningful to me as I ponder on what lies ahead for me in this life and what lies beyond this when all that remains here are cremains. It is a somber thought that I have outlived parents, a sister, and younger friends. Soon I will reach the four score years mentioned in the ninetieth Psalm. I often ask myself why I have lived this long. I guess God still has work for me to do here, before it continues in the beyond.

When I think about the afterlife, I feel like I have a split-screen (using computerized language). On one side is the religious heritage handed down from my parents, and on the other, my own faith forged through endless questions and struggles. Most of my life is history, so isn't it logical to think about the next journey of life? I resonate with the old Negro spiritual, "This world is not my home, I'm just a passing thro, My treasures are laid somewhere beyond the blue."[2] I love this life, and know that nothing is permanent here but love. Like both of you, I have many unanswered questions about the life after death and hope we share some of our speculations in future letters.

In the meantime, life remains an interim between this life and the next. I know too well that I am living on borrowed time. In West Virginia, I once saw a church bulletin board that caught my attention: "What

2. Brumley, "This World is Not My Home," lines 1 and 2.

on earth are you doing for heaven's sake?" Even in the evening of my life, I cannot get so heavenly minded that I forget this world. My world now is my family, here and scattered in three other states, and this community where I will be until my end.

I am still involved in a ministry to people with Alzheimer's disease or other forms of dementia. As I know myself, I realize I do this in memory of our mother, who died such an untimely death from a form of this disease. And yet, I have always stood with the outsiders and strangers of our society. I have tried to be there for them. I find God in these people, whose minds are gone, but whose souls are still within them. As Richard Bach said so well: "Here is a test to find whether your mission on earth is finished: If you're alive, it isn't."[3]

Keep the faith,

Richard

3. Bach, *Illusions*, 144.

November 1, 2008

All Saints' Day

Dear Brothers,

Tomorrow, November 2, is All Saints' Day and I will join the congregation at Fourth Presbyterian to sing, pray, and most specially, to ponder those loved ones who have "crossed over." As I thought on this today, while I "put to bed" my terrace garden (a sign of death and resurrection, but, now the finality of the dying plants is depressing), can we be like a plant seed and somehow spring to life again? One of my potted plants was a coleus that had enormous tubers when I pulled them up. I decided to keep some, large and small. I put them in a brown paper bag in our closet where it is dark most of the time. Next spring I shall bring them out after a winter of rest and, hopefully, they will root in the warmth of the sun and, again, flourish from May (that's Chicago) till November. I am told, though, that eventually the tuber will wear out and not blossom any more.

Is the tuber an analogy to the human form? I don't know, but it seems to me that we are so much more developed than a plant that something eternal must be about us. Perhaps because we have a mind we think too much about all this. Maybe a simple life form has an advantage over our infinitely smarter mind.

But, I know that sooner or later we will become, hopefully, a "saint": Saint Richard, Saint John actually sound pretty cool. But I wonder what Mary Ann, Pat,

Judith, Kax, Mother, and Dad do all day as "saints"? What's it like? Can it be like it is here or not? I suppose our minds and psyches are so locked in the gravity of our belongings and unless we're mystics, we can't get through to the saintly form.

These may be the "musings" of a seventy-three-year-old, but just maybe I'm beginning to perceive more clearly across that "thin line" the Welsh talk about. I do believe my experience with the seminary and encountering the poor and those without justice has given me a stronger view that there is an eternity. Sometimes simplicity is sublime. Thursday, I wore my Chicago Theological Seminary robe for the first time since becoming a doctor. Our new President was installed and the moment of grace came to me when Joanne Terrell, a professor, sang "Great is Thy Faithfulness" with an ad lib clarinet contribution by Rev. Ozzie Davis and a piano that sounded like a revival meeting in Indiana. Eternity? Just for a moment I could see across the thin veil and experience the "saints": Pat, Judith, Kax, Mother, Dad, and Kim—what a thrilling moment! Was it ancestor worship, DNA coming through, sentimentalism? I prefer to accept the knowledge that I was, at that brief moment, at one with the saints.

Peace brothers,

Howard

November 7, 2008

Dear Brothers,

Here it is at 5:30 in the morning and it is "deathly dark," as the saying goes. Strange, but what flashes through my mind is a picture of our father every morning at a very early hour in the bathroom shaving, shaving cream all over his face, with a cigar dangling out of his mouth, and the sounds of the morning news drifting from a radio in his office. No wonder that when I smell a cigar, I always think of him, and even sometimes when I am shaving and look into the mirror, I wonder whether it is him or me staring back. But the struggles between fathers and sons are the stuff of literature, so why am I an exception? Most sons begin by rebelling against their fathers and then later may learn to come to terms with them.

I, like you, Howard, often wonder whether those we love are still "alive" in some way we really can't know or even imagine. At times, like you, I sense what the poet Wordsworth called "intimations of immortality," a feeling that says we are more than our bodies and that something deep within does not die. But I admit I have no idea if these intimations are true or whether they are just my way of still not accepting death's finality.

Let me wax philosophical for a moment, after all, I teach philosophy, so bear with me. Philosophy is as much about death as it is life. When he was asked to summarize his philosophy, Plato said: "practice dying."

I think by that he meant to realize that ultimately life is very short and losses all too common, and that the philosophic mind understands this and seeks to live well, if not long. Facing death makes life more precious, each day a gift.

There are many schools of thought about what happens to the human personality after death. The first is that when we die, that's it. A second is that something in us, call it a "soul," survives the body and continues in some transformed way. Another view is that we don't die at all but that our soul returns to life in another form and keeps returning until we "get it right." Still a fourth view is that when we die we become part of that primary energy which created everything, losing our uniqueness, but becoming part of a greater reality. Then, of course, there is the Christian view that we were raised on and heard preached in our father's sermons. But, to tell you the truth, I am not sure what that view is any longer. I know the common view is that when a person dies, he or she goes straight to heaven or hell or perhaps spends a little time in purgatory, like detention after a school day, and then, as a neighbor said to me, "goes to talk with Jesus." I must confess, however, that I've been reading the stories and sayings of Jesus anew, and while I find some references to this kind of view (ironically, the thief on the cross, the "unbeliever," was told by Jesus he would enter paradise because of his faith), I think the clearest understanding is that when we die we "sleep," and are awakened only by the voice of Jesus, perhaps at the end of time. Dick, you're the New Testament scholar, what do you find that Jesus says about life beyond this one that are his words and not those of the later church?

As I finish writing these words I realize how limited our reason is to respond to the question of life beyond death. The truth is I have only hints and guesses and feelings about being in touch with those who have died. I don't really know what, if anything, awaits us after we pass from this earth. And, to be honest, I find myself turned off by those who use the promise of heaven or the threat of hell to "save our souls." Of course, as you know, we have our share of fire and brimstone preachers in our family tree, so perhaps I am rebelling against them.

What I always come back to are metaphors or stories that point to realities we cannot express any other way. Howard, your metaphor was about the plant in your garden, the dying it must do over winter before being reborn in the spring. That's a good metaphor. Sometimes I imagine a great banquet, a homecoming celebration if you will, where all those I love who have passed from this life are gathered. It's like one of our family reunions. There is a lot of food and laughter and stories about our lives—the good times and the not-so-good ones. It's a pleasant and enjoyable time. Whether it points to something beyond what I can know now, I am not sure.

The morning light is breaking outside. I can see the yellow and red leaves and hear the train whistle sadly calling in the distance. Another day has dawned and I am here to see and hear. Maybe that's enough.

I am, after all, a rather fragile human creature in the midst of a life that is far greater than my own.

Shalom,

John

November 25, 2008

Dear Brothers,

After reading your last letters about life after death, I deeply appreciate your keen insights. Yet I find it difficult to write at all about life after death at this juncture in my life, for I am focused now on mourning and moving beyond a small death in my life. However, in a later letter I will write more on this subject. But after all, as the poet T. S. Eliot once wrote about life after death, all we have are hints and guesses. In fact, the more I read and think about life after death, the less I know. It is a leap into faith to believe. Frankly, after studying this subject for some time, I am content to accept Jesus' promise that he has gone to prepare a place for us, and where he is, we will be someday.

As you both know, as the oldest son of the fourth generation Morgan preachers, I was programmed to follow our British tradition: enter the ministry and become G. Campbell Morgan II, which Dad could not accomplish in his life. So, as the eldest son of the fourth generation he picked me to become his substitute. Earlier in my life, I knew that I had been scripted to follow the Morgan way, but that was mere intellectual awareness, without an understanding of all the complex issues that made me the tragic family scapegoat. I did not fully realize that as the oldest son I would be expected to carry on the Morgan religious tradition. I became the only one to try and achieve the impossible and then miserably failed and caused baggage I carried for far too long.

I can lament now the fact that I had lacked the courage to follow my own dreams and become a sportswriter. I envisioned myself in some press box watching endless games, and then writing great sports stories. The melody I had composed for my life was not played. But there was no sense in keeping the keyboard closed. Then and now I have tried to find new songs to sing in teaching, pastoral care, and writing. But to live in that past and to be stuck there like concrete is self-defeating and terribly depressing. It is time to find closure and move onward from this significant, but small death.

I can see clearly now how both parents were the victims of authoritarian fathers, and could do no less than lay that burden on me. For these reasons and others, I now accept them but I admit it is hard to forget the hurt they inflicted on me and my siblings with that silent hostility that enshrouded our home, a daily presence, blowing over us in *cold* gusts. I accept the fact that Dad programmed me for a life career I never chose, and caused me to forfeit a career I had chosen. Small deaths involve mourning your losses, and then moving on. In the quiet of the chapel where I live, I have mourned these losses of an unhappy childhood and the small death of my broken dreams. I can now move beyond there and then to here and now.

All losses of life involve relinquishment, trust, and then transformation and new beginnings. I hope now to move beyond all the baggage of family dynamics and find new beginnings, even at the eleventh hour of my life.

As to hints of life after death, nature does provide some analogies. Jesus talked about the kernel of wheat that had to fall to the ground and die to produce a harvest. Paul used the analogy of the seed of corn sown in the ground. The seed dies in the dark soil and becomes a full-grown plant, an ear of corn. Christians have always used the butterfly as a symbol of the resurrection. Though the butterfly may seem too flimsy a metaphor for such a subject, it makes sense to me. It is concealed in the winter in a tightly hidden shroud, and then is remade. By the time its chrysalis breaks, the caterpillar has changed from a crawly, woolly creature to a winged flash of color, a butterfly, which climbs very high and is lost in the sun—such a glorious transformation.

Over fifty years ago, in a seminary class taught by Dr. Balmer Kelly, I became aware that the forty days between Easter and the Ascension are our only hold on eternity. When we are dead, we are dead, not disembodied spirits who fly into the unknown, or souls who return to this life to "get it right." Our clue is the Christ whose identity was the same yet totally different. What happened to those who saw this reality would be like finding an old friend so changed that we walk right past her, and do a double take when we finally realize who she is. In the language of paradox there is continuity and yet discontinuity. Beyond death, God raises our whole personhood—mind, body, and spirit—to a new reality. So it well may be that in the afterlife we may not know our loved ones at first, but something of who they were will ignite a fire of recognition within us as we join them in a glorious celebration and homecoming.

Years ago, John, you introduced me to two books. Miguel de Unamuno's *Tragic Sense of Life* meant so much to me in my struggle for faith. The other book, Herbert Butterfield's *Christianity and History*, offered a powerful conviction: "Hold to Christ and for the rest be totally uncommitted."[4] So I hold to this risen Christ as my one sure hope. All for all other speculations and theories I am totally uncommitted. But my faith will not be realized until I see "face to face and understand even as I am fully understood" (1 Cor 13:12). I truly believe one day the sadness and brokenness of our dysfunctional family and my dreams denied will be healed by love, always stronger than death.

That's where I am now, trusting God for the future, and trying to work through this small death to a new beginning, and being a "resurrected person" where I live, a place where aging debilities, dementia, and death exist close at hand every day. My new beginning will involve no lofty hopes of success or approval by others, but simply doing small things with great love.

Live in the audacity of hope, brothers,

Richard

---

4. Butterfield, *Christianity and History*, 146.

December 23, 2008

Dear Brothers,

Yesterday afternoon, as the sun was setting over snowy Chicago, I stood by Judith's grave in Graceland Cemetery just off Clark Street above Wrigley Field. Strange images, too—the lights at Wrigley were on as they built the ice rink where the Black Hawks will play on New Year's Day. The subway rambled by in the distance—life, motion, and activity. Yet in the quiet of a late winter afternoon, all was still and desolate.

Somehow I was transfixed by the end of it all—nothing but a marker with Judith's name, dates of birth and death, and mine with the birth date. It seems so totally unfair that Judith and Pat aren't here to see their grandchildren, to say nothing of Kim to see her children grow and blossom. It was downright depressing standing there, and I felt totally helpless, not to mention cold in the snow.

Is it possible that Judith, Pat, and Kim are all the "communion of saints" and in an eternal way, part of what I am experiencing in this holiday season? Here I am at the age of seventy-three, yet Pat died at fifty-five, Judith at fifty-eight, and Kim at forty-two. I think about the years they have missed, or at least we have missed them. It seems completely unfair.

The Christmas holidays are a hard time for me remembering what might have been. And yet, for me, it feels like three lives—dying twice with the loss of Pat and Judith and rising again to new life and happiness, today with Brooks and before with Judith. Can it be that the death of a loved one can also be a death of oneself, only to "rise again" in a different form yet the same?

I'm puzzled and pleased at the same with what I have managed to do with my life so far, especially with eleven grandchildren and how I impact their lives. And yet, when I die, what is there? Are there just memories of my being with family and friends, or do I have an eternal existence? Perhaps it is enough to know that my person will survive in the minds of others, especially family and friends. I am generally pleased with the way I have lived and shared what I have. At times I've been criticized for my generosity, but I would not change one thing I've done. And there's so much more to do!

Maybe that's one definition of eternity—to do good acts and serve as an example for others.

Back to Graceland Cemetery—one-third of my ashes will rest there at some point. What of it? Is there any difference in having been here? Is there a way I can continue to be "in the world" beyond life? I sure would like to find a way. It's such a blast living!

So, for now, I shall keep on keeping on, using my life and experience to live fully. What comes later will continue to be a living project to figure out.

Merry Christmas, brothers, and I do so value our brotherly friendship.

Howard

December 27, 2008

Dear Brothers,

You've both given me a great deal to think about in your last letters. As the "black sheep" of the Morgan flock, let me play devil's advocate for a moment. I know you will bear with me even if you don't agree. To be able to converse with others, especially my own brothers, is a rare opportunity, particularly when it comes to the matter of death, about which few speak openly and honestly. I am glad that here at least I can express openly what I feel and think.

Howard, I remember after Judith's death, your confiding in Richard and I how she did not believe there was anything beyond this life. At the time I thought how hard it must be for those who survive to think she was no more. And yet, during her memorial service at the chapel in Chicago, listening to others speak in an almost Quaker-like way about Judith, I had a new sense of appreciation for her courage, for telling it like she thought it was and not using pious platitudes about "going home to Jesus" or coating over the grim reminder of life's limitations death always brings. I felt a sense of kinship with her stance because it was brave and those of you who knew and loved her let it be so in the service.

Lately, as I near my own three score years and ten, death has become closer. I think after my surgery about two years ago when I almost died, the reality of death has somehow gotten more real. And yet, honestly, I am less fearful, not because I am convinced there is a life beyond this one (what person is crazy enough to believe that an eternity with one's self would be bearable?), but because I don't feel I will die without having fully lived. "When it's time to die, let us not discover that we have never lived," wrote Thoreau. And even with all my false starts and failures, I have lived the best I knew how. A lot of people who fear death really fear the unfinished business of their lives.

Lately I've gotten hooked on a television show called *House.* I don't often turn to popular culture for philosophy, even theology, but I love this show because its main character, Dr. Gregory House, is such a truthful character—crazy like a fox, Socratic, and in some ways almost "Christ-like" (he would rage at this suggestion). He tells the truth, sometimes brutally, often without being sensitive to others, but still honestly, the way I wish I could be. Dr. House is especially blunt when it comes to what others say about death and life beyond. House is an atheist: he doesn't believe in heaven and he isn't that thrilled with life here either. The only thing he says in this regard is that our reason is the only quality that separates us from animals. And when we die, we just die and are gone.

In a recent episode, "97 Seconds," a patient believes in the afterlife and tries to kill himself to get there. The paramedics said he was "technically dead" for ninety-seven seconds, and the patient said, "it was the best ninety-seven seconds of my life." House can't stand this: "Okay, here's what happened. Your oxygen-deprived brain shutting down, flooded endorphins, serotonin, and gave you the visions." In the same episode a dying cancer patient tells House he can't wait to get out of his body. "Get out and go where? You think you're gonna sprout wings and start flying around with other angels? Don't be an idiot. There's no after, there is just this," says House. Later, House's co-worker Wilson chides House and tells him he doesn't know anything about heaven because "you haven't been there." To which House responds: "Oh God, I'm tired of that argument. I don't have to go to Detroit to know that it smells!"[5]

I may not be as cynical as House, but I feel a sense of relief that someone can be as honest and clear about this as he can. I don't want to be some spirit leaving my body and looking for the light at the end of a tunnel. I have no desire to spend eternity with people I can't stand being around for five minutes in this life. And I am repulsed by the promises of religious charlatans who promise eternity if others will strap a bomb inside their coats and blow up innocent children and also those who promise eternal life if they will simply confess Jesus as their savior.

I hope on my deathbed I can still be clear, even rational. If there's something beyond this life, I am not afraid. And if there is nothing, I have at least lived an interesting life and made some difference. Who knows, maybe we can continue our discussions on

5. *House*, "97 Seconds."

the other side of life? If not, these letters are at least worthwhile now.

Shalom,

John

December 31, 2008

Dear Brothers,

An old year is dying and a new one about to be born. Your last letters prompted some real thought about what I believe about the life beyond. Faith demands doubt, for without doubt, faith becomes gullible acceptance of platitudes, or "believing a million things before breakfast."

There remains a healthy reticence about what lies beyond. Maybe that is well and good, for we all need respite from the fiery preaching about heaven and hell. As the old spiritual wisely says, "Ev'rybody talkin' 'bout heav'n ain't gwine there."[6] Yet, everyone wants to go to heaven, but very few ask about it. Most of us are repelled by some of the images in current thought. I, for one, do not want to sit on a soft cloud, eternally strumming a harp (I didn't even learn to play the piano in this life) or being bored doing nothing. But the question persists, "What will happen when I die?" At my age, that is more than curiosity, it is a vital question. One of my friends died, and I said to my wife as I grieved his loss, "Now he knows." I don't.

Will we sleep in the grave, as Billy Graham believes, until Christ returns to this world and snatches all his followers from the graveyards of the earth and allow those who remain to join them in the great escape? Or when I die, will my lifeless soul become part

6. Author unknown, entitled "Heav'n, Heav'n" or "Going to Shout All Over God's Heaven."

of the "all soul" of the universe? Or is death a transition from this life to the next, a journey of remarkable delight and discovery?

What do I believe now? I believe that as Christ was in the forty days between Easter and the Ascension, so my person will be transformed in a twinkling of an eye. Like Christ, I will not be subject to time or space. I can go wherever I wish, and I can't wait to revisit the white beaches of Iona, and the thin place at Tintern Abbey in endless adventures of the new life. However, although I will experience a glorious reunion with loved ones, and be embraced by light, there will need to be a time of further growth before I can attain the light perpetual as did saints like Francis of Assisi, Gandhi, Lincoln, and Mother Teresa.

German theologian Helmut Thielicke told a story about two medieval monks who also struggled with what lies beyond this life. They made a pact between them, that whoever died first would return the next night, and in answer to the question *Qualiter* (what is the other world like), he would answer either *Taliter* (same as we thought), or *Aliter* (other than we thought). One of the monks died and the next night he appeared as a ghost to his brother monk, who anxiously asked, *Aliter?* The answer was, *Totaliter Aliter* (totally different).[7]

So it must be for me. I can speculate, dream, and imagine all I want about what life after death will be like. Really all I can hope for is that it will be so totally

7. Freburger, "A deeper clerical problem," para. 27.

different, that I will be lost in wonder, love, and praise. The words of Paul come to mind, "No eye has seen, no ear has heard, and no mind has imagined what God has prepared for those who love him" (1 Cor 2:9).

My phone just rang; a call from the charge nurse in personal care called. An aged resident is terribly depressed and wants to die. She has suffered loss after loss, and there is no hope of getting better. She wants to talk with me and I cannot give Ruth assurance that she will be healed in this life. But I can share with her my belief that there is a life beyond this one, where all our brokenness will be healed and we will be whole persons.

Stay tuned,

Richard

February 20, 2009

Dear Brothers,

It seems ages since we exchanged letters. We have been more focused on the issues of this world than questions about the next one. We live in a time when people are losing their jobs, and scrambling for any work to put food on the table. We see the hopelessness on many faces that mirrors the pain in their hearts. I cannot tell any of my friends who suffer in this economy that it's going to get better soon. Nor can I submit to what a church bulletin board next to us said: "The retirement plan is out of this world." We have to live in this world.

However, this past week two more of my friends who live here died. Where are they now? Where will I be when my name appears on that memorial board? On Sunday we sang a hymn in church, and the last verse raised the question I can't escape.

> Finish, then Thy new creation;
> Pure and spotless let us be.
> Let us see Thy great salvation
> Perfectly restored in Thee;
> Changed from glory into glory,
> Till in heaven we take our place,
> 'Till we cast our crowns before Thee,
> Lost in wonder, love, and praise.[8]

Have my friends who died "taken their place in heaven?" I confess I feel trapped between a hell I don't believe exists and a heaven I can't possibly imagine.

8. Wesley, "Love Divine, All Loves Excelling," stanza 4.

I have struggled with this, and have come to believe there is a "time beyond time" between this present existence and the future life. I know, it sounds like the Roman doctrine of purgatory, and when the Protestant Reformers discarded this belief, we may have thrown out the baby with the bathwater. Such a "time beyond time" will not be punitive, for I have long since thrown off my childish belief that God is a nasty policeman who is out to get us and send us to hell.

Many religions believe that we will get a second chance to get it right through an endless cycle of life-death-rebirth. I can accept that these cycles do occur and have occurred in my lifetime. But I cannot accept that this rebirth after death will take place on this earth. Nor can I agree with the view of New Testament scholar N. T. Wright, that at death we enter "restful happiness" as we wait for the resurrection of Christ at End Time. When we leave "time" we enter "eternity," and what we anticipate may already have happened.

Dante's Middle Kingdom intrigues me. Pilgrims constantly make their way up the Mount, in a continual process of getting rid of whatever in their mortal lives weighs them down or blinds them to the light. They make this journey in the embrace of God's love, not seeking "salvation," but "holiness" as they approach heaven.

Two analogies may help explain what I mean. Ellis Island, New York, was a naturalization center where new arrivals from the old country became citizens of America. We need such a "holding place," where we can rid the "ego" in our lives and then be free to become citizens of heaven. Or, think of a trapeze artist swinging through the air, always protected by a safety net. She cannot fall to her death, but neither can she quite reach the heights she wished. So, for us, when we die, we are always kept safe in the love of God, but not quite able to meet God.

Recently, I had to work through a difficult time of depression, which involved freeing myself from some knots of the past. It was a time of despair, almost a small death. All my achievements were forgotten, and I suffered the annihilation of everything I knew and thought myself to be. Only through this "hell" did I find God's mercy. Could not this "time beyond time" after death be a continual process of emptying ourselves of selfishness so that God can fill us with love? All I know is I have soul work to do in this life which will continue after death until I am conformed to the image of God in Christ Jesus.

I will be more than interested in your response to this view in your next letters. Forgive me for being too curious about what happens at death. In two weeks I will be eighty years old, and can't escape wondering what will happen when I close my eyes in death. This much I do know: what I may think is a *conclusion* to my life will become a *commencement,* and nothing can separate me from the love of God.

So, I muddle on in this life, and the rest that may be when I die is simply not up to me.

Hopefully,

Richard

[NOTE: Howard has been on the road for some time and will rejoin our conversations when he is able. Meanwhile the letters continue between Richard and John.]

March 1, 2009

St. David's Day

Dear Brothers,

It seems appropriate in many ways that I write this letter today, St. David's Day, the Welsh holiday celebrated around the world. It was while we were in Wales a few years ago that I became more aware of a different understanding of life and death and the "thin places" where the veil separating the two might be lifted for a glance or two. It was sitting under an old oak tree early one morning while on a walk above Tintern Abbey that I became aware of a different, deeper dimension breaking into our time. I wouldn't be surprised at all if centuries ago other inhabitants of that land felt the same.

Sometimes thinking about eternity leads to confusion about the meaning of time. Eternity may not be an extension of time but rather the absence of what we think of as time altogether. After all, scientists estimate that most of the universe is made up of black holes where there is no time at all. And I learned that it might be possible to catch a glimpse of eternity on this side of death, whether it is sitting under an old oak tree or listening to music or reading a poem. Eternity is the timeless bumping into us living in the prison of time and space, and we need not wait to see if there is anything beyond death.

Our way of thinking I have come to understand is too limiting, or as a theologian long ago wrote in a book noted: our God "is too small." Perhaps, if you will pardon the inference, thinking about life after death only for those who are Christians is too parochial. God is bigger than our religions and, I hope, more generous than those who say there is only one way to heaven.

The other day while teaching a class I realized that there were at least four different traditions among the students, each representing a different understanding. A Hindu and Buddhist in the class thought karma ruled a round of rebirths, a Moslem something different, and even among the Christian majority in the class there were differing opinions about whether there was a hell and about who goes there or heaven. It dawned on me that our understandings of life beyond life are often shaped by the tradition in which we grew up, our parents' beliefs, our culture, the age in which we live.

I think of all this today on St. David's Day as I look at a Celtic cross I brought back from Wales. The cross looks different, though it is clearly a Christian one. However, rather than appearing to be a cross with the vertical longer than the horizontal, each portion of the cross is the same—almost four equal pieces pointing to the four directions of ancient religion. What is intriguing are the interwoven knots shown in the Celtic cross, combining the ancient pagan Welsh symbol with the

Christian one. What has happened in my symbol is that later Christians took an older "pagan" symbol and used it for their purposes.

I guess my point is that there are many understandings of what happens beyond death, and some that indicate nothing. And for some reason I take some comfort in those pre-Christian ancestors of ours, part of what some have called members of "primary religion," who could simply infer from nature some basic wisdom—life begins, struggles, dies, and perhaps may be reborn. And we do not need a book, spiritual leader, or even organization to know this much—all we need do is open our eyes and hearts to what is always here. In a strange way this is a comfort to me—God or the Creator is more generous than we are, and gives us daily reminders of generosity. If God is so generous in this life, then I have no difficulty inferring that this characteristic stretches beyond death. But I really don't need more these days than to know the daffodils in my garden even now are getting ready to rise from the ground. I await them eagerly.

In brotherly affection,

JohnnybyGod (the name I chose in Wales)

March 17, 2009

Dear Brothers,

It is hard to believe but I saw some signs of spring in this cold, northern wasteland. I spied one crocus struggling to break out of the crusted earth, and I remember the Zen saying that when one crocus appears it is spring all over the world. Yesterday, it was so nice I took a walk outside with my trusted cane and actually heard robins chirping their songs of spring. However, it will be a while before most of the bulbs my wife planted are either brave enough or crazy enough to emerge from the snow-crusted ground. In a real way I feel cheated by this northern climate, especially since I lived almost fifty years in the South and hear about some of my southern friends wearing short-sleeved shirts, admiring the flowering trees, and basking in the sun.

As I meditated on the coming warmth and pageantry of spring, I confess I admit I was wrong about some past beliefs. For years I had waged a vendetta against those who used the spring of the year as a symbol of the resurrection of Jesus. After all what do chocolate bunnies, marshmallow chickies, and dyed eggs have to do with God's miracle of raising Jesus from the dead? I saw no connection between the advent of spring and the Easter story. After all, the word Easter comes from the Teutonic goddess of spring, Oestre, which surely had no connection with Christ's resurrection.

Now, a little wiser and perhaps mellowed by age, I see a connection. It was on a warm, spring day when the women found the stone rolled from the empty tomb. Jesus did not rise from the dead in the fall of the year when everything was dying, and frozen leaves stuck to the ground. Nor did this event happen in the winter, when cold and misery show no signs of life. It was spring, when God's world comes alive, that Jesus burst from the tomb.

One day last week we sang a new hymn that reso-nated with what I am saying.

> In the bulb there is a flower; in the seed,
>   an apple tree;
> In cocoons, a hidden promise: butterflies
>   will soon be free!
> In the cold and snow of winter there's a
>   spring that waits to be
> Unrevealed until its season, something
>   God alone can see.
>
> In the end is our beginning; in our time
>   infinity;
> In our doubt, there is believing; in our
>   life, eternity.
> In our death, a resurrection: at the last a
>   victory,
> Unrevealed until its season, something
>   God alone can see.[9]

Jesus said very little about life after death, but he did use an analogy to give us an example: " . . . Unless a grain of wheat falls to the ground and dies, it remains

9. Sleeth, "Hymn of Promise," stanzas 1 and 3.

just a single grain; but if it dies, it bears much fruit"
(John 12:24). This is similar to the analogy Paul used
about the seed put into the ground. The outer husk
of this seed simply rots away, but within this seed is
a germ of life that is raised up with a completely new
plant around it. From nature, we learn that after death
there is continuity of identity with us as we are now,
but a different form of the new life.

Most New Testament scholars think Mark ends
in this way. "So they [the women] went out and fled
from the tomb, for terror and amazement had seized
them, and they said nothing to anyone, for they were
afraid" (Mark 16:8). We can speculate all we want
about what did happen on that first Sunday of a new
world, but like the women, I know I would be scared
out of my mind if I had been there. I would have been
speechless, too scared to tell anyone what I had experienced. That's why Mark's account, the earliest of all
the gospels, has the ring of reality about it. If the gospel
writers had constructed a factually consistent account
of that spring morning, I would have been suspicious
they had made it up. But the fact that no one discerns
a consistent account where all the gospels agree on the
events of Easter witnesses to the fact that something
awesome had happened. For them, life would never be
the same.

A young boy asked me about life after death when
his grandmother died. I recalled the fable of the water
bugs that scurried over the soft mud at the bottom of
the pond. At times a member of their colony would
climb the stem of a pond lily and vanish. They were

concerned as to what happened to them, so they agreed that one of their colony when he climbed the stem of the pond lily, would return and tell the other bugs where it went. But when he rose from the water, he noticed a dramatic change in his body: he had become a dragonfly. Remembering his promise, he tried to go back, but realized he couldn't return, and his friends would have to wait until they became dragonflies.[10]

There is something profound in this simple story. We feebly struggle on this side of the pond, but, beyond us, our loved ones have winged off happily into a wonderful new world of sun and air. Now, I must go outside and see if any new bulbs have broken from the ground.

Spring Is Coming,

Richard

10. Stickney, *Water Bugs and Dragon Flies*.

March 24, 2009

Dear Brothers,

I believe you are aware that Brooks and I have escaped the bitter winter in Chicago to seek the warm weather of Florida for March. Early this morning I went to our sun porch overlooking the Gulf of Mexico. It was a brilliant morning with perfect temperatures in the seventies and a warm breeze off the water. I felt unusually content and alert to the warming world around me. I gradually felt a very strong presence of those who have passed beyond, especially those loved ones who have died in my generation: Pat, Mary Ann, Judith, and especially my daughter, Kimberly Joy.

Actually as the light becomes more brilliant and intense my loved ones appear to me, in my line of vision. Their presence evokes strong memories of our days together; one by one, episodes float before me, as the sun gets stronger and stronger. Holidays, times at the Jersey Shore, marriages, and graduations: it's really hard to describe, in words, these moments. It's like trying to verbally report on what happens to my conscious, connecting to my subconscious, in hearing and feeling the Chicago Symphony performing Mozart or Bach. Or the "presence" I encounter when I look into the eyes of a grandchild, seeing Pat or Judith (or myself for that matter).

Moments like this remind me why I am still here to represent those loves ones to their families and friends. I feel such a strong kinship to these departed family members of my generation. It's different than the older generations who have died. Yes, I remember them and am so thankful for them, but I don't feel the need or the responsibility to represent them in quite the same way as I do with those who have died in the next generation.

Anyway, pleasant thoughts on a beautiful day. It often surprises me on a bright day like this one how my mood and consciousness are lifted. Maybe it's a reaction to the wintry months in Chicago where the sun rarely shines. When it does, the local population all seems more alert and happy. But, deeper than that, light for me, and I suspect for most people, does evoke a clearer vision of life than darkness. Goodness, I've seen dark times, and happily, many more lighter times. I've learned from both, but it's the light that evokes a sense of eternity and peacefulness, a realization that a place or state of mind and soul undoubtedly does have reality. I am convinced that our loved ones who've "passed," as our African-American brothers say, are well and far happier than I can possibly imagine. As our dad said, quoting Scripture as we drove away after Mother's death: "In the twinkling of an eye . . . we shall be changed" (1 Cor 15:52). So be it.

And the beach beckons.

Cheers,

Howard

March 26, 2009

Dear Brothers,

As I near another birthday and close in on the biblical mark of seventy birthdays, I am becoming more skeptical of all the great truth claims from creatures of such limited intelligence who seem capable not only of destroying another nation but the entire planet. I am optimistic about the courage I find in individuals, but pessimistic about the collective wisdom which seems hell bent on sending others to purgatory or worse simply because they believe something different.

Richard, I resonate with your understanding of what is always in front of us and which we seem to miss—life's incredible renewal of itself. I don't know if that points to any life beyond death for us, but it sure does point to the magnificent processes of nature, as close as my back yard or even more wondrous in pictures of other galaxies from the Hubble telescope.

I also believe there is a kind of arrogance among us for thinking that we are so important that individually each person will go on forever. I'm not sure I want to live forever and I sometimes think it takes a lot of gall to think otherwise. Maybe this is it—the life we have now and for however long—and we'd better make the most of it, not just for ourselves but others.

I don't think any of us really knows for sure what will happen after we die. Maybe nothing, maybe something, but unless we've been there and returned, we can't really know. Even those who have had near-death experiences don't really know—they testify to seeing a light and a tunnel, common reports, but some who study this phenomena claim it has more to do with the release of chemicals in the brain than life after death.

I also realize that the whole question of justice arises when one looks at the issue of life after death. If there is no life after death, then life sometimes seems unfair—the good suffer and the evil prosper; and there is no final judgment. I accept that life is unfair, but I am not sure it makes it more palatable by claiming heaven as life's final arbitrator. What if there is nothing beyond this life yet people spend all their time thinking there is? Isn't that what one of my friends called "pie-in-the-sky religion," taking our energies away from fighting for justice here and now?

As I near my sixty-eighth birthday next week, I am finding a sense of solace believing this: that if there is something beyond this life, I am not afraid; and if there is nothing, I have lived a full life and will simply fall into a deep and forgetful sleep.

Keep your eyes on the returning birds and daffodils and those nearby you love. So either say, "Praise spring" or "The Lord has risen."

John

April 5, 2009

Palm Sunday

Dear Brothers,

I sit in the pew at Tabernacle Presbyterian in Philadelphia as a silent observer and my thoughts go beyond children waving palms and happy songs to the deep darkness of Good Friday. Somehow I cannot seem to share the wild celebration of that first entry into the city. I remember that the palms will soon become the ashes that remind us of suffering and death. One of the hymns that we sang was "Ride on! ride on in majesty! In lowly pomp ride on to die."[11]

I like the title of David Shield's recent book: *The Thing about Life Is That One Day You'll Be Dead.* There are times when I visit the cemetery where my cremains will be buried and I think of the poem by John David Burton, "When Everyone Comes Back from the Cemetery Except Me,"[12] and that stark reality hits me in the face: our culture still continues to deceive us with its refusal and denial of death. The learned scholar Samuel Johnson said that he never had a moment when death was not terrible to him. Yet, it seems life remains one long effort not to think about it.

Even when innocent people are gunned down in New York, when casualties in Iraq increase, when policemen are murdered by a white supremacist, and when

11. Milman, "Ride On! Ride On in Majesty," stanza 2, lines 1 and 2.

12. Burton, "When Everyone Comes Back from the Cemetery Except Me."

a young baseball player is killed by a drunk driver, we prefer not to think about death, especially *our* death. As I now see the view from eighty years on earth, death becomes more real every day. I read obituaries from my college and seminary bulletins and cringe as I notice how many of my friends and classmates have left this life. Indeed, in the midst of life, we are in death. I often wonder how I will die, and pray it will not come at the end of a lingering illness, but rather, sudden, like a thief in the night.

It seems to me that we all really die alone. Loved ones may be at the bedside, but the paradox is, the closer you come to death, the further away they will be.

A memory of a play I read years ago comes back to me: Eugene O'Neill's *Lazarus Laughed*. After four days of clinical death, Lazarus returns to his daily tasks and yet he is changed; he has become a non-anxious person, no longer vulnerable to the fear that diminished life. He laughs all the time. At the last when he stands before the Roman emperor, convulsed with laughter, the emperor says to him, "You have a choice. You'll either stop this infernal laughter or I'm going to put you to death." Lazarus continues to laugh and says to the emperor, "Go ahead and do what you will. There is no death. There is only life."[13]

I love the scene in the movie *Field of Dreams* when Terence Mann leaves the field and walks into the cornfields and laughs. No wonder Luke expressed the feelings of the first disciples after the resurrection as "they still disbelieved for joy, and wondered" (Luke 24:41).

13. O'Neill, *Lazarus Laughed*, act 3:2.

I will never forget the moment six years ago when we got word that Mary was near death. We sped across the Pennsylvania Turnpike in record time and just made it as she passed from this life to the next. Even now I remember the look of sweet peace on her face as she stepped into the next world. Nor will I forget when I stepped outside the door of her house into the evening shadows; there was a gentle warmth and silence.

> Death is not extinguishing the lamp;
> it is putting out the light because the
>   dawn has come.
> Rabindrath Tagore (1861–1941)

Richard

April 11, 2009

Dear Brothers,

Perhaps it is appropriate that I, the skeptic, am writing one day before Easter, a day that remembers the death and resurrection of Jesus. I think I am perhaps closer to the original disciples in many ways, most of whom fled from the cross believing their teacher was gone. At least this is what Mark reports in what most scholars believe to be the earliest account. Isn't it ironic that it is the women who first come to the tomb (and who are now denied becoming priests in some traditions) and then who come and tell the fearful disciples, who still refuse to believe them?

I will not be sitting in a church pew on Easter, nor will I miss doing so, except perhaps the combined voices of a great choir. I certainly don't miss the sermons. And I won't go for the sake of appearances or simply to feel good. It still seems to me that many Christians I know are in Christendom, as the Danish thinker Soren Kierkegaard described it, and like the disciples of old, still don't get it. I *know* I don't get it, but I also know there are some things I do get, even if they fall outside what Christians deem important today.

I do understand that Jesus was a teacher and activist who went around the countryside for a few years criticizing the religious leaders of his time and the political ones as well, and preaching the nearness of God in the presence of the ordinary events and people of his time. I do get it that Jesus turned the tables upside down in every way imaginable, including the tables of the moneychangers in the synagogue. And he turned the tables of the power brokers upside down, too, teaching nonviolence and concern for the oppressed as the marks of his kingdom rather than the conquest of foreign countries or the might of government. And I think that if Jesus were to return today he might be hard pressed to find anything left of what he taught. I agree with a teacher I once learned from who said that Jesus preached the kingdom of God, and the early church preached Jesus.

Perhaps the empty tomb symbolizes what I find now on my faith journey. Something happened. What happened, I do not know. And, in a similar way, I also go to the empty tombs of all those I have known who have passed beyond this life to what someone once called "The Great Perhaps." Maybe one day I will find out.

Bora da,

John

April 12, 2009

Easter Sunday

Dear Brothers,

As we agreed, we would terminate our exchange of letters with our wishes for what happens when death comes. In the first place, I definitely know what I do *not* want, either at a memorial service or regarding the disposal of my remains. I have been involved in far too many funerals as a pastor and visitor to know that I shudder at some of the pagan practices I have observed.

As to these questions, let me describe a funeral I attended a few months ago in a small western Pennsylvania town. The town had been decimated by the shutdown of steel mills years ago and the deserted streets and blank faces made you think of death. Mournful music was piped into the parlor as a few of us gathered to pay our respects to a gracious lady who had lived ninety-seven years.

Her mortal remains were "laid out" in a coffin as one woman remarked, "Doesn't she look better now than when she was alive. I am so glad she chose such a pretty dress for the viewing." I slumped down in a chair, trying to avoid looking at the shell of what had been a vibrant lady, and wondered what all this had to do with resurrection. We sang "Abide with me; fast falls the eventide; the darkness deepens; Lord with me abide. When other helpers fail and comforts flee, help of the helpless, O abide with me."[14] After a few words were spoken, the funeral director told us the service would be concluded at the grave. Very little mention of her life was said, or even some words of hope. I left feeling terribly sad and depressed.

Some time ago I wrote out my own wishes for my end of life. I can only trust that my wife and family will keep them as a sacred trust.

Richard

14. Lyte, "Abide With Me, " stanza 1.

Final Wishes

At death, I will be cremated after any organs have been donated to the living. There will be no body to be "laid out," or viewing of a coffin. An inexpensive urn is enough for my cremains. There will a private burial ceremony at the St. Clair Cemetery Greensburg, Pennsylvania, where plots of ground have been purchased in a quiet area at the back of the cemetery. I have requested (if possible) that my brother, Dr. John Morgan, and an old friend, Dr. Donovan Drake, officiate. Only immediate family will be at the grave. At an appointed time a memorial service (see below) will be held at the First Presbyterian Church, Greensburg, Pennsylvania, officiated by John Morgan and Donovan Drake. A luncheon and reception will follow in the church fellowship hall, for the benefit of family and friends. My wife will place copies of my books on a table with a few photos. That matter I leave to her and my family.

At the Grave

Readings: Robert Weston, *Cup of Strength*; Words from the music of *Les Miserables*

Commital of Ashes to the Ground

Memorial Service

Music: Johann Sebastian Bach (selected by my wife)

Hymns: "I Greet Thee Who My Sure Redeemer Art"; "Joyful Joyful, We Adore Thee"; "For all the Saints"

Readings: Psalm 121; Psalm 139; 1 Corinthians 15:50–58

Also:

> Perhaps they are not the stars,
> bur rather openings in heaven
> where the love of our lost ones
>   pours through
> and shines down upon us to let us
>   know they are happy.
> (Intuit Legend)

Brief Comments on the Life of Richard Lyon Morgan:

John Crossley Morgan, Howard Campbell Morgan, Donovan Drake, and other designated family members (including grandchildren)

Prayers for Those Who Mourn (Please include the following):

> We give back to you, O God, those
> whom you gave to us.

You did not lose them when you
    gave them to us,
and we do not lose them by their
    return to you.
Your dear Son has taught us that
    life is eternal and love cannot die.
So death is only a horizon and a
    horizon is only the limit of our sight.
Open our eyes to see more clearly, and
    draw us closer to you
that we may know that we are nearer to
    our loved ones,
who are with you. You have told us that
    you are preparing
a place for is; prepare us also for that
    place, that where you are,
we my also be always.
O dear Lord of life and death.[15]

At the closing of the service before the final bene-
diction, I request that my son, Randy Morgan, sing the
song of committal from the Catholic funeral mass:
"Saints of God, come to his aid." (Music Included.)

If possible, the Welsh song (two verses) "Nos Da"
may be sung or read, or the song, "Do Not Be Afraid."

---

15. Penn, untitled prayer.

April 25, 2009

Dear Brothers,

I must admit it feels strange, but necessary, to think about one's own memorial service, yet I know from doing so many as a minister that leaving it up to family and friends to create the service can cause consternation. I have always felt how much better it would be if the deceased had left his or her own desires for the service and not burdened the family or friends who are already walking through the valley of the shadow of death and confused and grief stricken.

Avoiding death is a great pastime, especially in a materialistic culture like ours that prides itself on possessions. Facing death means realizing that in the end it is not one's possessions that matter most but the other qualities of life one grows through suffering and joy—compassion, love, self-respect, honesty, and leaving behind something of worth far more valuable than money.

I've just looked again at my will and am glad to see I have on file a declaration that I want no extraordinary means to keep me alive. But here is what I filed nearly twenty years ago as my wishes for a service. I debated changing them, but if I do that now I will probably continue until my deathbed and I wouldn't wish that on anyone around. My memorial service, like my life, has improved over the years but is far from perfect, and I suspect if there is another side to this life, I will continue to learn. I can't think of anything more boring than an eternity of one's self.

Before the actual service I would appreciate having a few close friends and family gather over a dinner and just talk about each other and, from time to time, me. If I am still around in some spiritual form, I urge those gathered to be careful. I would not want to be someone haunted by my ghost. Of course, though I am the youngest there is no guarantee I will last the longest on this earth, so if one or both of you remain after I am gone, please send a few words of hope to be read at the service.

Here is actually what I wrote some decades ago and which I have filed with my will:

In the Quaker form of service, I'd like people gathered in a circle, perhaps only a vase of flowers on a table in the middle of the circle. I'd like the service to be short, no more than a half hour. It should open with some piano music, perhaps Mendelssohn's May Breezes, op. 62, no. 1, and then close with J. S. Bach, Prelude in C Major. I want people to sit quietly for a few moments after the prelude. Then anyone who wishes can read anything they want or speak, hopefully about my life not my death.

If my wife Cynthia is willing to sing something, I would love that, as I would if any of my children wish to read something they have written or to sing something.

And then I would simply like people to have a good time: eating, telling stories, and most especially laughing. Who knows, I might be there and they'd better follow my instructions!

In the best of all worlds, I'd love to have my ashes tossed in the river by Tintern Abbey in Wales; the river has always seemed such a fit symbol for the deeper meanings of life; but, given the reality of cost, I'd settle like my sister Mary Ann to have my ashes tossed in the Atlantic Ocean near Barnegat Light, New Jersey.

Bora da,

John

P. S. On Friday, a doctor told me I have a suspicious growth on my arm that will need to have a biopsy. It is probably nothing, but it is a reminder that death is never gone and as Socrates said long ago the wise person knows this and lives life to the fullest when he or she has it.

May 9, 2009

Dear Brothers,

You've encouraged me to outline what I'd like for my memorial service. It reminds me of Dad's organist, "Melody Mac," at Chambers-Wylie who composed and recorded the music for his own service. Dad said it was eerie, I hope mine produces a better feeling. At least I won't be there to speak or sing!

I've had more than my share of family services, so I'll select, in my opinion, the best of them for me and add to them.

I'd like a traditional church memorial service (no body or casket, please) at Fourth Presbyterian Church with John Buchanan and Susan Thistlethwaite as pastors. The service should start with the hymn, "For All the Saints." One other hymn should be sung: "The Lord's My Shepherd" (Scottish Psalter 1650 tune; melody by Jesse S. Irvine 1836–1887). And the service should finish by the organ playing Handel's "The Hallelujah Chorus."

I'd like a full twenty-minute expository sermon by John (or Susan) on the text Proverbs 3:6 with reference to our family tradition of fathers passing this text onto their children.

I'd also like a solo from Handel: "I Know My Redeemer Liveth."

No pallbearers permitted.

Hopefully, all my seven children and eleven grandchildren (or however many there may be at that time) will attend and sit up front with Brooks and the two of you with your spouses. Pat and Drue as well, if possible.

I will provide a list of those to be invited to a gathering afterwards which will be attached to my will, lodged at Sidley and Austin, a Chicago law firm (John McDonough, partner). I'd like this event to be a party with refreshments (including food, wine, and spirits) held at Spiaggia in its private dining room for all attendees. With appropriate music of a joyful, not subdued nature. My life should be celebrated and, if the spirit moves anyone, I can be "roasted" freely.

In addition, the evening before the memorial service I'd like to have the family group gather at our apartment and sit and chat about their experiences with me, and what they learned about living from me. Refreshments should be served, catered by Mary Mastercola of La Petite Folie in Hyde Park. Susan, Dow Edgerton, and the two of you should be there to facilitate the conversations (I found the evening with Kim's family so helpful, and Judith's service with a circle of friends remembering her to be the best experiences I've had at these affairs). No funeral home or "visitation" please.

Since I plan to be at all these events, although unseen by all, I will carefully monitor what is said. And, like African religions, I will be able to reward or punish those speaking depending on the nature of their remarks and, perhaps, reveal who Dad meant when he said, "except one who has been a bitter disappointment."

I suppose the point of all this is to leave the same way I lived, surrounded by family and friends in the comfort of the church tradition in which I was raised and lived my life.

My remains are to be cremated and the ashes divided into three parts: first for burial in Arlington Cemetery, Upper Darby, Pennsylvania, next to Pat's gravesite; second at Graceland Cemetery in Chicago next to Judith's ashes; and last to be given to Brooks who may follow her own desire to be placed next to her when the time comes or be scattered in the ocean at Harvey Cedars, New Jersey, or in the Gulf of Mexico at Boca Grande, Florida.

I'm not positive how I will react or feel when I'm about to leave this earth in death and indeed afterwards. However, I believe and hope I will feel fulfilled and not regretful of things undone and that I will be at peace with the faith by which I have tried to live, some times more truly than others. I am confident that "the other side" will be as beautiful and lovely as the spring day I just experienced on my walk along Lake Michigan with blooming tulips and happy passersby.

Cheers and God Bless,

Howard

Postscript

August 14, 2009

Dear Brothers:

It has been nearly a year since we began this exchange of letters about facing death. I know writing them has not been easy; facing one's death never is. But I have learned that preparing for one's death is really preparing for one's life. When we realize our time is limited on this earth we tend to value those closest and dearest and spend our hours more wisely.

None of us really know the precise date and time of our passing from this earth, nor can predict with certainty what, if anything, awaits us on the other side of life. Hopefully these letters will provide comfort to those we love who are left behind and some measure of wisdom to those we don't know who also must pass through this valley of the shadow of death.

If we meet again on the other side, each of us has often joked that we have a few questions for those who went before, questions we have been unable to have answered on this side of the great divide. Nothing would give us greater joy than to sit around a table talking about what it's really like on the other side.

Until we meet again (possibly),

John

Bibliography

Bach, Richard. *Illusions*. New York: Delacorte Press, 1977.

Brumley, Alfred E. "This World is Not My Home." Alfred E. Brumley & Sons, 1965.

Burton, John David. "When Everyone Comes Back from the Cemetery Except Me." In *Naked in the Streets*. Frankfurt, Germany: Ontos Verlag, 1985.

Butterfield, Herbert. *Christianity and History*. New York: Bell Publishers, 1950.

Freburger, William J. "A deeper clerical problem than sex—disbelief in life after death." National Catholic Reporter (April 16, 1993). Online: http://findarticles.com/p/articles/mi_m1141/is_n24_v29/ai_13685904/?tag=content;col1

House. "97 Seconds." Episode 403, first broadcast 9 October 2007 by Fox Network. Directed by David Platt and written by Russel Friend and Garrett Lerner.

Lyte, Henry Francis. *Lyte's Remains*. London, 1850.

Milman, Henry H. "Ride On! Ride On in Majesty." In *Hymns written and adapted to the Weekly Church Service of the Year*. London: J. Murray, 1827.

O'Neill, Eugene. *Lazarus Laughed*. New York: Boni and Liveright, 1925.

Penn, William. Untitled prayer. In *The Communion of Saints*, edited by Horton Davies. Grand Rapids, MI: William B. Eerdmans Publishing Company, 1990.

Sleeth, Natalie. "Hymn of Promise." Carol Stream, IL: Hope Publishing Company, 1986.

Stickney, Doris. *Water Bugs and Dragon Flies*. Cleveland, OH: Pilgrim Press, 1970, 1997.

Tennyson, Alfred. *Demeter and Other Poems*. London: MacMillan, 1889.

Wesley, Charles. *Hymns for those that seek, and those that have Redemption in the Blood of Jesus Christ*. London: Strahan, 1747.